THE FAMILY MESSAGE BOOK

Dr Rie Natalenko

ISBN 978-0-9941732-6-3

For my family, who have always encouraged me to do what needs to be done. Thank you.

Thank you to all the people who read this and made such valuable suggestions.

Also, thank you to Julia Kuris, who has designed such amazing covers for me.

"All we have to decide is what to do with the time that is given to us." –JRR Tolkien

Dr Rie Natalenko, author of *The Family Memory Project* and *The Family Memory Kit,* has, for many years, been passionate about family history. She is an award winning screenwriter, novelist, poet and short filmmaker. She lives on the beautiful South Coast of NSW, Australia, with her husband and animals.

www.TheFamilyMemorySite.com

The Family Memory Project
Dr Rie Natalenko

The Family Memory Project will help you to gather, record and preserve your family stories. These memories are part of your heritage, something that you can share with your children and grandchildren.

The Family Memory Project is a step-by-step proven system that makes collecting your relatives' memories easy and rewarding.

It's the present of the past... for the future.

Table of Contents

The Family Message Book   9
What is this book for?   9
How to complete the book   11
Why are some things listed twice?   12

The USB   13
What is the USB for?   13
How to password-protect a USB drive   14

Date Page   15

About Me...   17
My Family   19
Other Important People In My Life   22
Family Tree   23
Timeline Of My Life   25
My Education And Working Life   27
Significant Events In My Life   30
Stories From My Life   31

My Personal World   33
My Interests And Hobbies: 35
My Pets   37
Special Friends   38
Regular Deliveries   40
Subscriptions: 41
My Will   42
Medical Details: 43
Guardianship: 45
My Important Documents: 46
My Vehicle(s)   49

Financial information   53
Insurance: 55
Personal debts and loans   61

Houses and properties   **65**
Other properties: *67*
If you rent your home: *68*

My Online World   **69**
Other social media accounts: *70*
Website(s)   *73*
Other online accounts: *74*
Email   *75*
Internet banking   *76*
Computer   *77*

My Business World   **79**
Business contacts   *81*

My Last Wishes   **85**

Special Bequests: **91**

Who Needs To Know?   **97**

Other Important Information: **105**
The Garden: *106*
Tradespeople you use: *107*
Recipes to pass on: *108*

Special Messages: **113**

Signature Page   **117**

The Family Message Book

What is this book for?

Last year three of my friends lost their last living parent.
One friend lost her husband.
At a time when their suffering was greatest, they had to sort out their loved one's affairs.
This was not easy for any of them, and their distress was made so much worse because they had no idea where to start.

This book will make everything easier for your family if you pass away.

This is your message to your family.

How to complete the book

There is a lot of information in the book, so don't try to do it all at once!

Over a few weeks, set aside half an hour a day and fill it in slowly.

Some bits will be easier than others. Do those first.

Some bits will not apply to you, so you don't need to do anything about those.

Some bits will change as the years go by, so write in pencil so you can change them.

Each year, on your birthday, go through the book and change the things that have changed since the last year.

Sign it and date it on the date page, every year.

If you enjoy this project, have a look at *The Family Memory Project*:
www.TheFamilyMemorySite.com

Why are some things listed twice?

You want to make this time easier for your family, so some information is listed twice, if it is relevant to two different sections.
This is because if your loved one is looking for specific information, they might not want to search through the whole book.

The USB[1]

What is the USB for?

The USB can hold spoken or video messages to your loved ones.

It should also contain a document which stores all your passwords.

Passwords which should go onto the USB are marked with an asterisk.

Some people may be concerned about writing passwords down in this book... and rightly so.

If you don't want to put this book in a secret place, or with your bank or your lawyer, it isn't wise to write passwords down.

If you put the passwords on a USB drive, it is possible to protect the USB drive with a password that only your family can know.

If you have a password to protect your USB drive, the information is much more secure.

---

1 If you have purchased a copy of the book without the USB and want to purchase a Family Message Book USB, please contact info@thefamilymemorysite.com.

If you can't do it yourself, get somebody you trust to help you.

- Plug your USB drive into your computer
- Right click (or control click on a Mac) the USB drive
- Scroll down to "password protect" or "encrypt"
- It will ask you to enter a password, and then confirm the password.

It may ask for a password hint (something to help you remember the password.)
If it doesn't ask you for a hint, write your password hint in the book, or on a label on the USB itself.

It is important that you remember this password, so the hint is VERY important. The hint should be something that your family would know, but strangers would not know.

For example, the hint could be:

Jamie's first dog (the password would be the dog's name)
Or
The church Marie was married in (the password would be the name of the church.)

Date Page

I filled in this book on:
_____(date) of _____ (month) _____ (year)

I made sure it was up-to-date on:
_____(date) of _____ (month) _____ (year)

I made sure it was up-to-date on:
_____(date) of _____ (month) _____ (year)

I made sure it was up-to-date on:
_____(date) of _____ (month) _____ (year)

I made sure it was up-to-date on:
_____(date) of _____ (month) _____ (year)

I made sure it was up-to-date on:
_____(date) of _____ (month) _____ (year)

I made sure it was up-to-date on:
_____(date) of _____ (month) _____ (year)

I made sure it was up-to-date on:
_____(date) of _____ (month) _____ (year)

I made sure it was up-to-date on:
_____(date) of _____ (month) _____ (year)

I made sure it was up-to-date on:
_____(date) of _____ (month) _____ (year)

I made sure it was up-to-date on:
_____(date) of _____ (month) _____ (year)

I made sure it was up-to-date on:
_____(date) of _____ (month) _____ (year)

I made sure it was up-to-date on:
_____(date) of _____ (month) _____ (year)

I made sure it was up-to-date on:
_____(date) of _____ (month) _____ (year)

About Me...

Full name

Previous names

Nicknames

Any interesting stories about how I got my name

Address

Town and country where I was born

Town and country I live in now

Main occupation

Spouse/Partner(s)

When and where married (If you were married more than once, list them all.)

My Family

Father's name

Father's address
Father's phone
Father's email

Other information

Mother's name

Mother's address
Mother's phone
Mother's email

Other information

My children / dependants
(Names, addresses, phone numbers, email)

Guardians of my dependants (Names, addresses,
phone numbers, email)

My siblings (Names, addresses, phone numbers, email)
You may like to mention your relationship with your various siblings.

Other Important People In My Life
(Names, relationship to me, address, phone number, email)

Family Tree

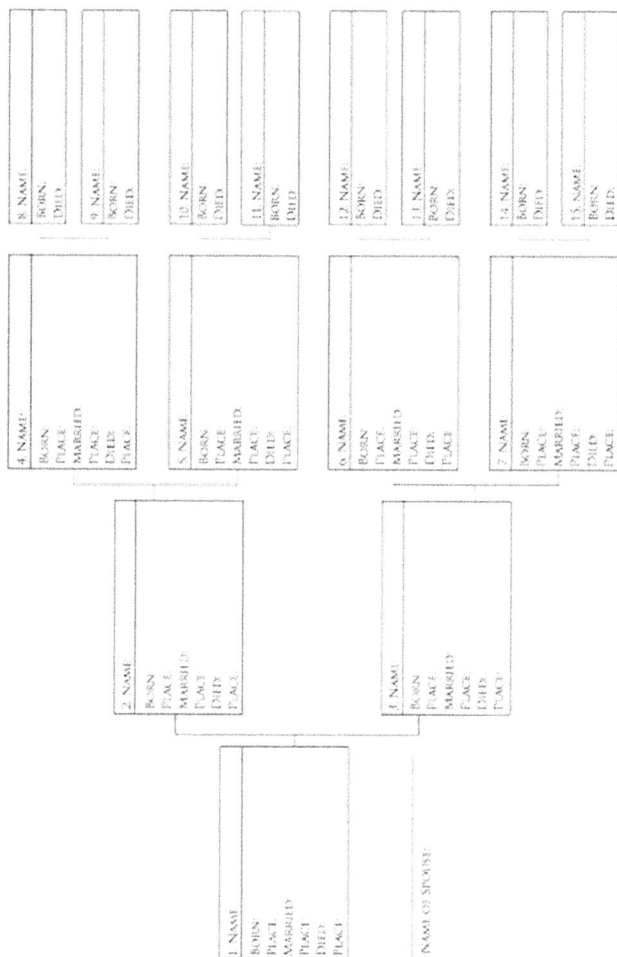

Timeline Of My Life

The Family Memory Timeline

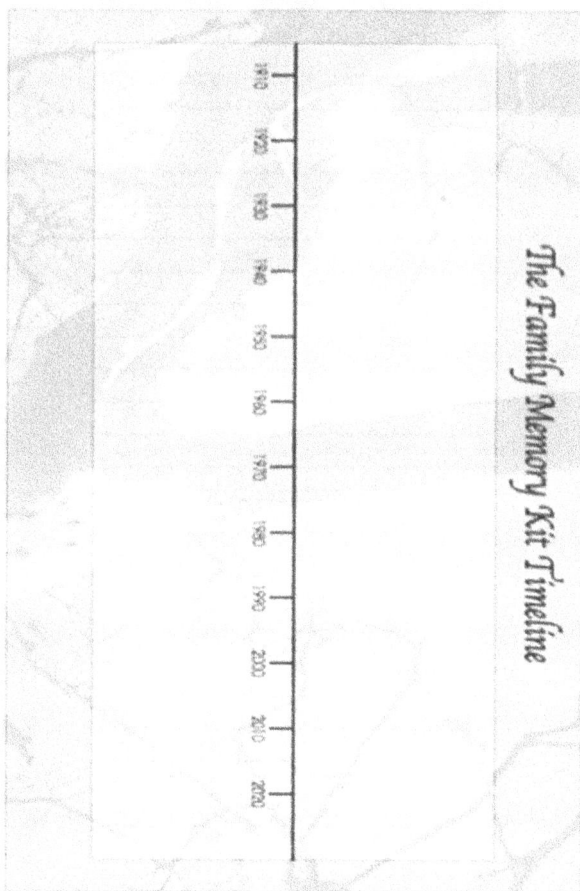

The Family Memory Kit Timeline

Where I studied
(primary schools, secondary schools, tertiary institutions)

Qualifications (where they were from, and when I earned them)

Languages spoken:

Where I worked (years and places)

Significant Events In My Life

Stories From My Life

Stories continued…

Stories continued…

Stories continued…

My Personal World

My Interests And Hobbies:

Clubs I belong to:
(membership number, contact name, contact details, positions held with years)

Institutions I belong to:
(membership name, contact details, information, position)

My Pets

Names of my pets:

Special requirements for the pets (feeding schedule, medications, what they like and dislike)

Vet contact information:

Who I would like to look after my pets:

Special Friends

(names and contact information)

Regular Deliveries
Types of deliveries and contact information

Subscriptions:

Name of magazine, institution, etc and contact information for cancellation.

My Will

Name of my Executor and contact information.

My will is kept here:
(contact information)

Copies are kept here:
(contact information)

Medical Details:

These are the important medical issues that have arisen in my life:

My Doctor is:
(Name, contact information)

My medicare number is:

My health fund is:
(Membership number, level of cover, contact details)

43

My specialists are:
(Name, contact information)

Guardianship:

I am guardian of the following people:
Names, addresses, contact details)

My Important Documents:

Passport 1, number
location:

Passport 1, number
location:

Marriage certificate, number
location:

Birth certificate, number
location:

Driver's licence, number
location:

Pension number:

Medicare card, number
location:

Land Rates notices, (name of council(s) and contact information.)

Electricity (name of provider, customer number, contact information)

Gas (name of provider, customer number, contact information)

Water (name of provider, customer number, contact information)

Telephone landline (name of provider, customer number, contact information)

Mobile phone (name of provider, customer number, contact information)

Internet (name of provider, customer number, contact information)

Post office box number and contact details. Where do you keep the key?

Other

Other

Other

My Vehicle(s)

Car
Type of car:
Date of purchase:
Registration:
Expiry:
Registration name:
Vin:
Loan information:

Location of relevant documents:
Insurance: (company, number)

Greenslip: (company, number)

Other (second car, boat, motor bike etc)

Type of vehicle:
Date of purchase:
Registration:
Expiry:
Registration name:
Vin:

Loan information:

Location of relevant documents:
Insurance: (company, number)
Greenslip: (company, number)

Other (second car, boat, motor bike etc)

Type of vehicle:
Date of purchase:
Registration:
Expiry:
Registration name:
Vin:
Loan information:

Location of relevant documents:
Insurance: (company, number)
Greenslip: (company, number)

Other (second car, boat, motor bike etc)

Type of vehicle:
Date of purchase:
Registration:
Expiry:
Registration name:
Vin:
Loan information:

Location of relevant documents:
Insurance: (company, number)
Greenslip: (company, number)

Financial information

Business financial information
(who to contact about your pay, any important information that your family needs to know or your work needs to know)

Superannuation details (fund, number, where the documents are kept)

Banking
Names of banks and account numbers.

Online banking: Name of bank, username and password*

Term deposits:
Name of bank and numbers:

Scheduled direct debits

Credit cards:
(Banks, numbers, passwords*)

Bank safe deposit box (es) location and passwords*

Insurance:

Life insurance
(Provider, number and access details)

Funeral insurance
(Provider, number and access details)

House and contents insurance
(Provider, number and access details)

Car insurance
(Provider, number and access details)

Greenslip
(Provider, number and access details)

Superannuation fund(s)
(Contact details, reference number)

Other insurance:
(Provider, number and access details)

Investments portfolio
Access details:

Financial advisor
(contact details – phone, email)

Stockbroker
(contact details – phone, email)

Shares
(details, contact person with contact details)

Solicitor
(contact details – phone, email)

Location of my will

Copies of my will

Power of Attorney.
(This person has the legal authority to look after your affairs on your behalf.)
Name
Address

Phone
Email

Tax
Accountant
(address/ phone/ email)

Personal tax file number

Company tax file numbers (names of companies)

Personal debts and loans

Debts:

Name
Phone / contact
Amount owed
Date
Reason for debt

Name
Phone / contact
Amount owed
Date
Reason for debt

Name
Phone / contact
Amount owed
Date
Reason for debt

Name
Phone / contact
Amount owed
Date
Reason for debt

Loans:

Name
Phone / contact
Amount of loan
Date
Reason for loan

Name
Phone / contact
Amount of loan
Date
Reason for loan

Name
Phone / contact
Amount of loan
Date
Reason for loan

Name

Phone / contact

Amount of loan

Date

Reason for loan

Houses and properties

Address

Title deed location

Purchase price

When purchased

Mortgage debt

Financial institution

Utility suppliers:

Electricity

Gas

Water

Council name (for rates)

Insurance details (numbers, amounts, insurance providers, contact details)

Alarm system details (provider, code*)

Other properties:

Deeds (location, names):

Address

Tenant
Lease
Contact number for tenant
Agent contact details

Rent

Mortgage details

Utility suppliers:
Electricity
Gas
Water
Council name (for rates)

Other details:

If you rent your home:

Name of landlord:

Address:

Email:

Phone number:

Weekly/monthly rent:

Bond amount:

Location of the rental documents:

Any other details or agreements:

My Online World

Computer password*

Social Media

Facebook (pages, username, password*)

Twitter (usernames, passwords*)

Pinterest (usernames, passwords)

Google plus (usernames, passwords*)

Other social media accounts:

On the next page is a list of the more popular online social networking sites. If you have accounts with any of these, write down the name of the site, your username and your password*.

43 Things

About.me

Academia.edu

Advogato

aNobii

AsianAvenue

aSmallWorld

Athlinks

Audimated.com

Bebo

Biip.no

BlackPlanet

Bolt.com

Busuu

Buzznet

CafeMom

Care2

CaringBridge

Classmates.com

Cloob

ClusterFlunk

CouchSurfing

CozyCot

Cross.tv

Crunchyroll

Cucumbertown

Cyworld

DailyBooth

DailyStrength

delicious

DeviantArt

Diaspora

Disaboom

Dol2day

DontStayIn

douban

Doximity

Draugiem.lv

Dreamwidth

DXY.cn

Elftown

Elixio

Ello

English, baby!

Eons.com

Epernicus

eToro

Experience Project

Exploroo

Faceparty

Faces.com

Fetlife

FilmAffinity

Filmow

FledgeWing

Flickr

Flixster

Focus.com

Fotki

Fotolog

Foursquare

Friendica

Friends Reunited

Friendster

Fuelmyblog

FullCircle

Gaia Online

GamerDNA

Gapyear.com

Gather.com

Gays.com

Geni.com

GetGlue

Gogoyoko

Goodreads

Goodwizz

GovLoop

Grindr

Grono.net

Habbo

hi5

Hospitality

Hotlist

HR.com

Hub Culture

Hyves

Ibibo

Identi.ca

Indaba Music

Influenster

Instagram

IRC-Galleria

italki.com

Itsmy

iWiW

Jaiku

Jiepang

Kaixin001

Kiwibox

Lafango

71

LaiBhaari
Last.fm
LibraryThing
Lifeknot
LinkedIn
LinkExpats
Listography
LiveJournal
Livemocha
Makeoutclub
MEETin
Meettheboss
Meetup
Millat
mixi
MocoSpace
MOG
MouthShut.com
Mubi
My Opera
MyHeritage
MyLife
Myspace
Nasza-klasa.pl
Netlog
Nexopia
NGO Post
Ning
Odnoklassniki
Open Diary
Orkut
OUTeverywhere
Partyflock

PatientsLikeMe
Pingsta
Plaxo
Playfire
Playlist.com
Plurk
Poolwo
Qapacity
Quechup
Qzone
Raptr
Ravelry
Renren
ReverbNation.com
Ryze
ScienceStage
Sgrouples
ShareTheMusic
Shelfari
Sina Weibo
Skoob
Skyrock
SocialVibe
Sonico.com
SoundCloud
Spaces
Spot.IM
Spring.me
Stage 32
Stickam
StudiVZ
StumbleUpon
Tagged

Talkbiznow
Taltopia
Taringa!
TeachStreet
TermWiki
The Sphere
TravBuddy.com
Travellerspoint
tribe.net
Trombi.com
Tuenti
Tumblr
Tylted
Viadeo
Virb
VK
Vox
Wattpad
WAYN
We Heart It
WeeWorld
Wellwer
Wepolls.com
Wer-kennt-wen
weRead
Wiser.org
Wooxie
Xanga
XING
Yammer
Yelp, Inc.

Website(s)

(Name of website,
URL,
URL of admin page
Admin username and password*
Website host
Control panel (c-panel) username and password*)
Name of organisation who manages your website
Contact name and contact details

Date that payment is due:

Other online accounts:

Paypal (username and password*)

Ebay (username and password*)

Other online shopping sites (e.g. Amazon, Coles online etc)
(Name of site, username and password*)

Email

Email provider
Email address
Username
Password*

If you have more than one email provider, or multiple email addresses, list all the providers with address, username and password.*

Internet banking

Name of bank (s)
Username
Password*

Computer
Password*

Login name

Important documents on my computer and passwords*
If you have password-protected documents on your computer, list the name of the documents, the location of the documents and the password.*

My Business World

Any business name(s) that you own:

List your ABN, ACN

Are you registered for GST?

Names, and access details for business accounts

Trademarks and patents

Business insurance (contact names, addresses, emails and access details)

Business contacts

Partners and affiliates who need to know.

Business contacts and colleagues who need to know.

Mailing list
(username, password etc for my mailing or
newsletter list)

Final email to my list/final newsletter/final blogpost:

My clients (The list may be too long to put in this book, but you should indicate here where the list is kept.)

Final message for my clients:

My book publishers (contact details etc)

Other business issues which should be addressed:

Electronic Lending Rights/ Public Lending Rights

My Last Wishes

Requests for my funeral:
This is the music I would like:

I would like a (religious or secular) service.

This is the venue I would prefer:

These are the funeral directors I would prefer:
(Name, contact details)

85

This is the celebrant I would prefer:

These are the customs I would like people to follow:

Anything else important about the service?

I would like to be (cremated or buried.)

I would like / I would not like my organs to be donated.

I would like to wear:

I would like notices put in the following papers:

I would prefer flowers or donations to (list the charity/ charities)

If you would like a certain photo to go on your coffin, put a copy on the USB or indicate its location:

Funeral insurance?
Insurer
Policy number
Details

This is what I would like on my headstone / plate

These are the notes for my Eulogy:

Notes continued...

Notes continued…

Notes continued…

Special Bequests:

If you have special things that you would like to leave to certain people, list them here.
Make sure you list the names and contact details of the people, and the description of the item.
Some people find it useful to write the person's name on a label and stick the label to the underside of the item.

If you have tools of your trade that you would like certain businesses or organisations to have, or items that you would like to be donated to a certain charity, make sure you list them here.

If there is something you DO NOT want to happen to your special things, write that here.

Special bequests continued...

Special bequests continued…

Special bequests continued...

Special bequests continued…

Special bequests continued...

Who Needs To Know?

List of people to contact:

If there are people who should be told first, then number the people after you have filled in the names here.

Don't forget to write in anyone who needs to know who is overseas.

Name/nickname:
Relationship/ friendship/business:
Address:

Phone:
Email:

Name/nickname:
Relationship/ friendship/business:
Address:

Phone:
Email:

Name/nickname:
Relationship/ friendship/business:
Address:

Phone:
Email:

Name/nickname:
Relationship/ friendship/business:
Address:

Phone:
Email:

Name/nickname:
Relationship/ friendship/business:
Address:

Phone:
Email:

Name/nickname:
Relationship/ friendship/business:
Address:

Phone:
Email:

Name/nickname:
Relationship/ friendship/business:
Address:

Phone:
Email:

Name/nickname:
Relationship/ friendship/business:
Address:

Phone:
Email:

Name/nickname:
Relationship/friendship/business:
Address:

Phone:
Email:

Name/nickname:
Relationship/friendship/business:
Address:

Phone:
Email:

Name/nickname:
Relationship/ friendship/business:
Address:

Phone:
Email:

Name/nickname:
Relationship/ friendship/business:
Address:

Phone:
Email:

Name/nickname:
Relationship/ friendship/business:
Address:

Phone:
Email:

Name/nickname:
Relationship/ friendship/business:
Address:

Phone:
Email:

Name/nickname:
Relationship/ friendship/business:
Address:

Phone:
Email:

Name/nickname:
Relationship/ friendship/business:
Address:

Phone:
Email:

Name/nickname:
Relationship/ friendship/business:
Address:

Phone:
Email:

Name/nickname:
Relationship/ friendship/business:
Address:

Phone:
Email:

Name/nickname:
Relationship/ friendship/business:
Address:

Phone:
Email:

Other Important Information:

On this page, list any important information that
others may need to know, such as:
how to use the oven or microwave,
where you keep the instruction books,
where you keep the spare key to the house

The Garden:

List here anything that people might need to know about maintaining the garden.
Which are the special plants?
Which need special care?

Tradespeople you use:

List here anyone that regularly maintains the house, garden etc. (contact details)

Recipes to pass on:

Do you have any family secret recipes?
Here is the opportunity to make sure that none are
lost.

Recipes continued...

Recipes continued...

Recipes continued...

Recipes continued...

Special Messages:

In this section of the book, place envelopes with any special messages for your loved ones.

If you wish, choose envelopes and paper that will mean something to them. You can place photos inside, too.

If you have something that they might like, and you wish to leave it to them, list that in the "special bequests" section.

If you have advice for certain special people, write it, and put it in an envelope for them.

If you have video messages for them, you can put those messages on the USB that goes with this book.

Place your messages here…

Place your messages here…

Place your messages here...

Place your messages here…

Place your messages here...

Place your messages here…

Place your messages here…

Signature Page

To the best of my knowledge, this is a true record:

Signature

_____

Date

_____

Updates and extras are available from:

www.TheFamilyMemorySite.com

You may also be interested in
The Family Memory Project
or
The Family Memory Kit.

www.ingramcontent.com/pod-product-compliance
Lightning Source LLC
Chambersburg PA
CBHW071945100426

42736CB00042B/2137